Success in Christ

Ministry and Business Devotional

Your First 7 Days

By Legenia M. Spiller-Bearden

"For I know the plans I have for you," declares the Lord, "plans to prosper you and not to harm you, plans to give you hope and a future."

Jeremiah 29:11

Copyright © 2016 Legenia M. Spiller - Bearden

Unless otherwise noted, all scripture is from the New International Version of the Bible.

THE HOLY BIBLE, NEW INTERNATIONAL VERSION®, NIV® Copyright © 1973, 1978, 1984, 2011 by Biblica, Inc.® Used by permission. All rights reserved worldwide.

Success in Christ
Ministry and Business
Your First 7 Days

All rights reserved.
ISBN-13: 978-0-692-81795-7 (Legenia M. Bearden)
ISBN-10: 0-692-81795-6

Printed in the United States of America. All rights reserved under International Copyright Law. No part of this book may be reproduced or transmitted in any form or by any means, electronic or mechanical, including photocopying, recording, or by any information storage and retrieval system, without the written permission of the publisher.

For more information about Legenia Bearden, visit
www.legeniabearden.com

Cover Photo Credit: Ronnie Woo Photography

I dedicate this devotional to my loving family & friends

My husband Daniel, children; Autume, Angelina, Theresa, Daniel Jr.

My loving mother Louise, brothers Andres and Derek

Special thank you to Shalonda.

My true friends

Thank you for every encouraging word and your presence.

I Love You All So Much!

How to Use this Devotional

Your First 7 Days

God has a plan for you today. As you begin your journey to owning a business or founding your non-profit organization seek God for guidance. Over the next seven days, read this "Success in Christ" devotional; after which pray and await instruction from the Lord. Listen to what the Spirit of God is telling you and write it down in the sections provided at the end of each devotional.

God is about to do something amazing in your life! Please share with me all of the great things God is doing through you at legenia@beardenproductions.com

TABLE OF CONTENTS

Introduction

Day One	Faith
Day Two	Time with God
Day Three	Prayer
Day Four	Courage
Day Five	Firm Foundation
Day Six	Listening
Day Seven	Expecting

INTRODUCTION

My faith made me do it; step out and believe God for what I could not see, but wanted so badly. Out of obedience to God I quit my job in June 2015 to run my non-profit organization; Bearden Productions Performing Arts Studio (BPPAS) full time…. without pay! Every day since then has been a beautiful, hard and rewarding experience.

Now I am blessed to be able to provide an amazing service to families in my community that otherwise would not have been able to participate in such programming; the performing arts! It is so fulfilling and I thank God every day that He chose me! I have never before been more fulfilled in my career and now I want to help others achieve the same sense of career satisfaction.

People often ask me how I got started and want to know what they can do to get their business off the ground. My first response always is "Seek God."

It is my prayer that this 7-day devotional will help you as you begin to seek God concerning your business. Maybe you have already started your business and just need encouragement. This devotional was created to do just that, give you spiritual guidance during the first 7 days of your new journey.

DAY 1

FAITH

Now faith is confidence in what we hope for and assurance about what we do not see.

Hebrews 11:1

Hebrews 11:1 sums it all up! I use to say this scripture often; it wasn't until I started my business that I truly understood its meaning. My experiences became my teacher. I literally had to give everything over to the Lord; I knew that I alone couldn't run my business; and that I NEEDED the Lord God just to get through a work day.

This is the way you must run your business; giving every part of your organization to God. Believing that He is who He says He is; that He will do what He says He will do. When you exercise your faith, God is moved and then He moves for you.

For so many, the problem with faith has been failure to totally surrender! Surrender your all to God so that He can take you to the next level; knowing that He cares for you and wants you to be successful, after all you are His child.

No, you may not know what the outcomes will be when you step out in faith. If you did, that wouldn't be faith now would it? Martin Luther King Jr. said "You don't have to see the whole staircase; just take the first step." I like this quote because too often people are afraid to take the first step. How can you ever have the business of your dreams, the business that God has already prepared for you, if you never take the first step?

Know that God loves you and is just waiting on you. So go ahead and make the first step today!

Prayer

Father, teach me to decrease so that you can increase in me. Increase my faith in you, help me to let go and let you operate in every aspect of my business and my life. Today Lord, I surrender to your will.

Faith puts God between us and our circumstances.
-Daniel Webster

God's Plans for Me Today:

_____
_____
_____
_____
_____
_____
_____
_____
_____
_____
_____

DAY 2
TIME WITH GOD

But seek ye first the kingdom of God and His righteousness,
and all these things shall be added unto you.
Matthew 6:33

Time with God is precious. Every morning when my husband leaves to take our daughter to school I turn off the television and the lights, put on some worship music and kneel before the father in prayer. During this time, I always feel God's presence throughout my home; it's always beautiful. All I do is weep and tell God how much I love Him, and how much I need Him to help me with the task He has given me. It is in my prayer times that I feel His love for me so strong and His anointing in me magnified. There is something about being in His presence that is like nothing on earth. My time with God reassures me, it gives me strength, it magnifies the spirit of discernment, and it prepares me for the day.

As you begin your business venture, set aside special times with God. Tell Him all that is in your heart, and wait for Him to speak. Your time with God is key, if you want to be led by Him.

You cannot do this alone! Put God at the forefront of this journey and success is sure to come!

Prayer

Lord I love you! I need and I want you! As I desire to draw closer to you make my ears sensitive to your voice, my heart long to be in your presence, and my mind stayed on you!

And let me take time for a quiet hour to spend, Lord, alone with thee.

- Kay Andew

God's Plans for Me Today:

_____
_____
_____
_____
_____
_____
_____
_____
_____
_____
_____
_____
_____
_____
_____
_____

DAY 3
PRAYER

But when you pray, go into your room, close the door and pray to your Father, who is unseen. Then your Father, who sees what is done in secret, will reward you.

Matthew 6:6

What is prayer? Prayer is communication with God, petitioning God, its sweet communion with God. There is no possible way you can expect to have success in your business if you do not talk to God on a regular basis. I am a witness! Prayer is the gateway to peace, reassurance, strength, and endurance. Every believer should always make time for prayer.

The late Pastor Charles H. Spurgeon said "Whenever God determines to do a great work; He first sets His people to pray." Don't you know there is a great work on the inside of you? This happened many times throughout the Bible. I'll give you two examples:

Nehemiah

Nehemiah saw a need and his first response was to fast and pray for several days. It was in prayer that he talked to the Father and was heard by Him. God gave Nehemiah favor when he went before King Artaxerxes, and he was able to perform the great task of completing the walls of Jerusalem.

Jesus

As our Lord and Savior prepared to give His life for us, He went into the garden of Gethsemane to pray. He knew of the great work set before Him and He was in agony over it. It was in His prayer time that the Lord sent two angels to strengthen and minister to Him.

Your time in prayer for your business allows God to hear your request and it allows you to hear the voice of God. Pray about everything concerning your business:

- Location of your business
- What bank to use
- What your slogan should be
- What your logo should look like
- Who to hire
- Who to fire

Ask God to be at the forefront of EVERYTHING concerning your business. David said in the book of Proverbs, *"Trust in the Lord with all your heart and lean not on your own understanding; in all your ways submit to Him, and He will make your paths straight." Proverb 3:5 & 6*

Prayer

Lord I need you to be a part of every facet of this business. I realize that it's not my business but it is your business. Help me to remember you in every decision-making process today. I submit to your will.

When man works, man works. When man prays, God works.

- William Carey

God's Plans for Me Today:

DAY 4

COURAGE

Have I not commanded you? Be strong and courageous. Do not be afraid; do not be discouraged, for the Lord your God will be with you wherever you go."

Joshua 1:9

Fear is not of God! It can only cripple you. This is why the book of Timothy says *"for the Spirit God gave us does not make us timid, but gives us power, love and self-discipline (2 Timothy 1:7)."* It takes courage to start a business; even more courage when you are unsure of yourself and your abilities. Remember when God commanded Joshua to take the children of Israel over to the promise land? He said *"every place that the sole of your foot shall tread upon, that have I given unto you…, starting from the wilderness…."* He said that once he (Joshua) got there *"no man will be able to stand before thee all the days of thy life: as I was with Moses, so I will be with thee: I will not fail thee, nor forsake thee." (Joshua 1:3-4)*

God can't give you what He's promised you if your feet aren't treading. You've got to take the first step. As you begin this journey to the promise, do not rely on yourself and your ability alone. God is the driving force behind your success. He has already equipped you with everything you need to have a successful business. But in order to get to that promise you must first have the courage to step out in faith and believe God at His word.

You can do this! You were born for this very reason. Do it today, do not forgo the greatness already inside of you because of fear. Look to the Father in everything you do, every decision you make and watch Him move in your business.

Prayer

Lord today I ask you for courage and strength as I step out in faith on my business venture. I realize that it is in you that I am successful, so I will acknowledge you today in all of my decisions and listen for your guidance. Lord I will obey.

Courage is grace under pressure.
-Earnest Hemingway

God's Plans for Me Today:

_____
_____
_____
_____
_____
_____
_____
_____
_____
_____
_____

DAY 5
FIRM FOUNDATION

Commit to the Lord whatever you do, and He will establish your plans
Proverbs 16:3

Build your business on a firm foundation, a solid foundation; and that is the Word of God! In the book of Luke Jesus says *"As for everyone who comes to me and hears my words and puts them into practice, I will show you what they are like. They are like a man building a house, who dug down deep and laid the foundation on rock. When a flood came, the torrent struck that house but could not shake it, because it was well built. But the one who hears my words and does not put them into practice is like a man who built a house on the ground without a foundation. The moment the torrent struck that house, it collapsed and its destruction was complete." Luke 6:47-49*

How do we build our business on the word of God? It starts with obedience. *"Commit to the Lord whatever you do, and He will establish your plans." Proverbs 16:3.* Merriam-Webster defines commit as: to put into charge or trust. So your job is to put God in charge. He is our direct supervisor and what He says goes. It is when we fail to obey God's commands that our foundation can begin to weaken.

When the foundation of your business begins with obedience to God, know that even in the darkest of times it will not be shaken.

Prayer

Father I realize that everything I have belongs to you. In your hands and care do I give my thought, ideas, hopes and dreams. Please give me an ear to hear what you are saying to me and give me a heart of obedience that I may please you.

Faith is the art of holding on to things in spite of your changing mood and circumstances.
-C.S. Lewis

God's Plans for Me Today:

_____
_____
_____
_____
_____
_____
_____
_____
_____
_____
_____
_____
_____
_____
_____

DAY 6

LISTENING

Consequently, faith comes from hearing the message, and the message is heard through the word about Christ.

Romans 10:17

In order to hear God, you must spend time with Him; time in prayer and time in His word. God speaks to us in various ways, but if you never spend time with Him how will you know His voice? The book of John says, *"My sheep listen to my voice; I know them, and they follow me. John 10:27."* Are you one of His sheep?

I have been with my husband for more than 12 years now; when he is in a crowded room talking with other people I can single out his voice alone, because it is familiar to me. When he touches me I know his touch because it is familiar to me. I even know how he will react to a situation before he even knows about it, because I know him. This is how God desires to be with us. We have got to get so close to God that we know His voice without a shadow of a doubt.

As you begin your business venture, and you do as I've stated earlier in this book; spend time with God, pray, have courage, and increase your faith. You've got to remember to listen. Often we will pray to God telling Him all of our problems and making request that we forget to simply be still and listen. I told you before that prayer is a conversation with God, but are we making it a two-way conversation or one where you are the only one speaking? God wants to talk too, and most importantly He wants you to listen.

Ways God speaks to us:

- Scripture – How many times have you opened your Bible just to find exactly what you needed?
- His servants – Has the Lord ever sent a word to you through another believer?
- Dreams – The Lord will often reveal things to us in dreams.
- Sermons – Nothing like a powerful message from the preacher that's just for you!
- His Creation – Nature, animals, the sky
- Music – Have you ever heard a spiritual song that just moved you?
- Prayer – Listen when you pray.
- His Spirit – Jesus said He left us a comforter, a helper, that is the Holy Spirit.
- Situations – God will allow our situations and circumstances to speak to us.

God has so much to tell you. Take out time to hear His voice, read His word and pray. Spend as much time as you can with the Father. I am a witness; the conversations will be the best you've ever had.

Prayer

Lord my soul cries out for a closer walk with you, to know you better so that I will know your voice when you speak. Give me, I pray, the ears to hear what your Spirit is saying and a heart to obey, without delay.

The most important thing in communication is to hear what isn't being said.
-Peter Drucker

God's Plans for Me Today:

_____
_____
_____
_____
_____
_____
_____
_____
_____
_____
_____
_____
_____
_____
_____
_____
_____

DAY 7
EXPECT

My soul, wait thou only upon God; for my expectation is from Him.
Psalms 62:5

This morning, wake up expecting something great from God. As you seek His guidance for your business, know that He is with you and has a plan for you.

Expectations are a belief that something will happen. Because you serve a God that can do the impossible, don't you know that there is nothing out of His reach? Your expectations from God are your faith in action. Though you may not see right now all that God has planned in terms of your success; know by faith that God has already met every need. Anything you need, His word says *He will supply (Philippians 4:19); not* only that, but Gods word also tells us that when we delight ourselves in Him, He will give us the desires of our hearts.

There is no need to fear, no need to fret, know that because of who He is and because of who you are in Him, you can expect the unexpected.

Prayer

Lord you are great, and greatly to be praised! I know that you have a plan for me; a plan for me to prosper, to have hope and a future. So today and everyday as I serve you I will expect nothing but greatness because you are a great God, able to do great things!

Success in Christ

Limit your thinking and expectation today to only the things God can do.
-Louie Giglio

God's Plans for Me Today:

IN CLOSING

Can I be honest? Starting a business will not be the easiest thing to do. There will be challenges, it will require an enormous amount of time and you may go through moments of despair. That is why this book was given to you. God wants you to know He is here for you. When God is in it, He makes the difficult times so much better.

"Be strong and courageous. Do not be afraid or terrified because of them, for the Lord your God goes with you; He will never leave you nor forsake you."
Deuteronomy 31:6

In times of hopelessness go to The Word of God; when you aren't sure where to turn go to The Word of God; when you feel as if no one is listening, go to The Word of God. I am a witness that He is already working things out for you.

My 30-day devotional will be available soon. I encourage you to get a copy and read it everyday before you begin your work day. Time in the Word will only encourage you, strengthen you and prepare you for your day.

I offer scriptures daily on my website and social media pages. Feel free to follow me on Facebook, Instagram and Twitter for your daily inspirations.

Lastly, I am here to pray with you. I love the people of God and desire nothing more than to help you as you take this huge step in your life. Feel free to email me, or message me on any of my social media platforms anytime you are in need of prayer.

Until next time my friends, may God bless you and keep you always.

Follow me on social media:

Facebook: https://www.facebook.com/legeniabearden/

Instagram: @legeniabearden

Twitter: @legeniabearden

Linkedin: Legenia M. Bearden

Website: www.legeniabearden.com

Email: legenia@beardenproductions.com

Bearden Productions Performing Arts Studio

A 501(c)(3) Performing Arts Organization

To make a contribution to Bearden Productions please visit us on the web at www.beardenproductions.com

Or call us at (501) 747-1036

Success in Christ
Ministry and Business
By Legenia Spiller-Bearden

www.ingramcontent.com/pod-product-compliance
Lightning Source LLC
Chambersburg PA
CBHW070052070426
42449CB00012BA/3238